SOVEREIGN

The floating island was never wanted.
Mortality reached it, dishonored its realms.
Judgement perished it with a single clause.
First I thought my fingers were blessed, wrung them dry with
raw appreciation.
The burning madness overflows, the air between eternity and I
Is deadly. Wondrous. Divine.
I have ceased to be. Glory was my last fleeting breath.
Dawn comes once again.

1. unwanted,

ESUM

i greeted you at midnight, our path's just crossing.
i reached out to touch you, a fleeting caress;
the tips of my fingers glowed like centuries of sand.
the power i could have, the fistful of hair begging to be cut…

and then you were gone, and my heart broke
like the hourglass of my thoughts. the sand trickled away.
power never came with my longing stare.

you were the worst of companions, with a key charmed
to fit any lock, open any cage i dared cast us in.
you had feet like mercury, stardust in your dazzling wake,
that i sank to my knees, bowed to the gods, and licked
till the streets were dull in their shine.

will you ever need me like i need you? are you content,
selfish enough to settle for the eternal shape of a flickering candle
in my mind, soon to be snuffed by expectation's endless tide.

the ink is running dry. give me a chance.
one day, i'll craft the mirror that makes you look back.
you will take that fatal second glance.

she dreams of
soaring past fluffy clouds
stopping only at the ninth.

"go no further," they will say,
"is it not already perfect?"   to the sun.

only it will never
be enough   closer
so she doesn't listen,
                                        and

only flies   closer

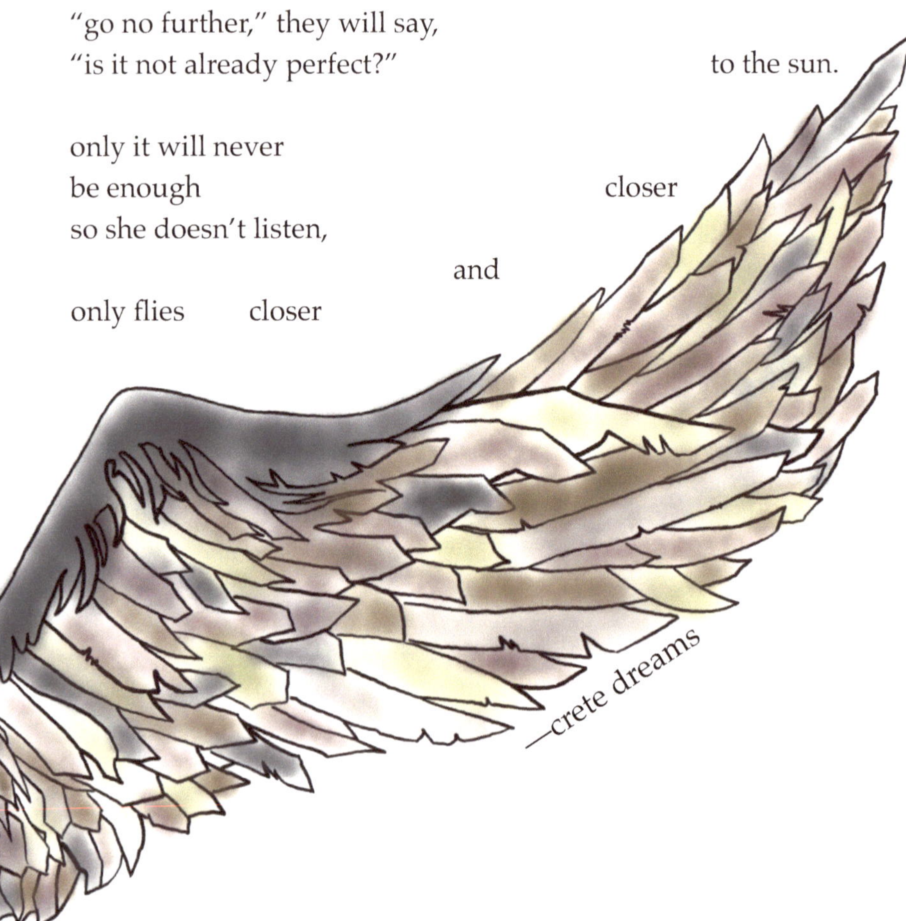

i'm in love with how it feels
when my heart is spilling
like the finest wine from my lips,
and no one accepts it
but a stack of loose-leafs
stapled neatly
like the collarbone that keeps you close,
holds you back from running from your skin
or shatters trying.

—a writer's lifeline

They show her the sun
and they show her the moon.
They offer a choice, under
which should she bloom

"You're bright as a blaze
and you're warm as a hearth.
We'll keep you protected,
just follow your heart."

She is but a child
and she asks them to wait,
so they pull her aside
and they show her the stakes.

"I'm sorry," she murmurs.
"I'm ruining the flow."
Her voice is like wind,
through their armor it blows

the warm off her skin
and the tan off her back,
a mural of hope
and they're painting it black.

Her coffee's now bitter
they're taking that too.
The stars in her eyes
dim to whispers of blue.

july

you pull me towards you, a paper straw
luckily drawn from the pile. your fingers
are delicate, perched on my skin.
i can taste the citrus on your lips.

praises paired with harsh breath, cubes of ice
that soothe the itch, shivered spines
as i cling to your chest, tugging
on your hair as if they were weeds.

the tip of your nose trails my neck,
and the seeds in my heart
start to grow like wine stains
on the bed. your tongue finds its mark.

i take a sip as doubt seeps into my being.
you lap at juice that overflows,
though it sickens your stomach
like the sweetest of poisons.

but you don't stop. you vow to never stop.

Our lantern hanging from the clothesline
Catches fire, the ashes scatter
Over my favorite shirt, stained green

The shared experience is your savior
Domestic quirks, a marriage in the works
It's the end of the world for me

The tightrope we share, it tenses in your favor
And frays for me, now personally
I'm horrible at balancing acts

They'd introduce me as fire breather
Blazes and burns, warrants concern
And yet my house stays intact

Until now. But no matter, it's fine
For we are all worms, waiting for the birds
And for some, the time comes a little earlier

Mirror Mirror

may all my enemies
glow like flawless topaz
and may the whole world
strive to twirl on their whims
so i will not look
at any one of them,
and see myself staring back
like the ugliest of reflections.

Dear,

The rivers ran dry until I cried & sang a perfect melody, a siren's scream for help that you listened to on repeat, seeking the meaning.

Did I lead you astray? Who wanted me more when I felt this way?

My death was not sealed, nor my hunger quenched by drawing from your well an image of perfection. Did I take your perfect vision, pirate at heart, make you quest through Hell to meet a double deception? For whom did I bleed? You will hate me when you begin to feel a pain, but know that it's a bucket merely catching my rain.

Please let her go, so I don't have to. Better yet, strike her down with a single kiss.

Yours.

HIS

i regretted taking you in
because your claws tore at skin
that was already scarred.

i regretted holding you close
because your purrs dislodged the prose
that i stored in my heart.

i regretted my good deeds
because the hand that always feeds
is often the next bite.

i regretted leaving you sad
because i was all you had
but then i saw

daylight.

We passed on the road, and time slowed.

We are all monsters, tinged green with envy,
and your irises swim with our reflections,
but we drown in those eyes, under twin inky skies,
and melt into emerald perfection.

Joan's godly arc never summoned such a spark,
such an ache, set ablaze like a saint at her stake.
You're an angel meant for flightless will,
a stranger sent to draw wings with lethal skill.

How did you entice the being
with hands that sculpted deities
to come to Earth every night
just to line your eyes with sable might?

What heavenly tool could control
that molten ebony, have it flow
like the tears you never cry
because you ride that endless high

of having perfect eyeliner?

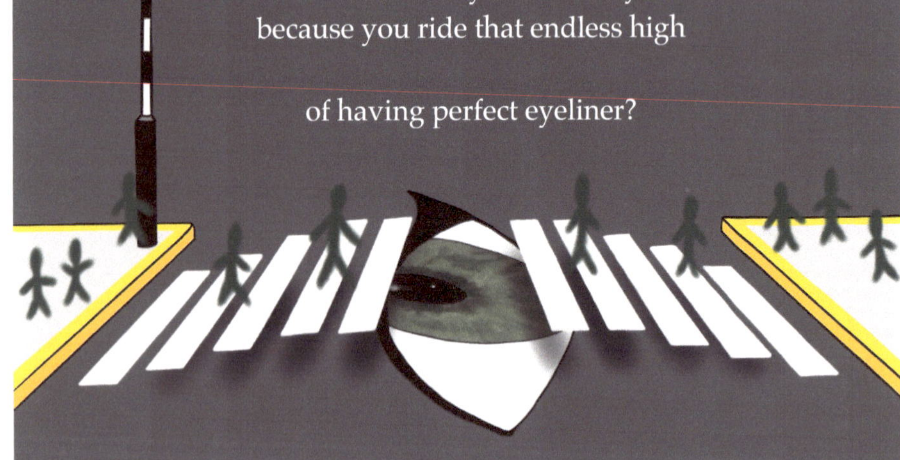

i feel like screaming
how is this fair?
why does he have the voice of angels?
why does she have diamond skin?
why do they have all the time in the world
at seventeen?
and what do i have?
a single good poem?
a paper wrist?
a cat with more lives than i?
the world is my pillow
and i don't know whether to dream
or scream

—overachiever

Strange Love

his smile was loud, her laugh was quiet.
that one's hair was tied back like a pirate.

devoted to all i see, i commit them all to ink.
his nails were blue, and her cheeks were pink.

their mock drawl, his chapped lips,
her leather jacket and swiveling hips.

his kindness, her pride,
their depression, fearless suicide.

every stranger i meet, i fall, and yet a hand to my chest
proves i never gave my heart away

after all.

Our wine glasses meet in a lifeless embrace
and I imagine the sound is something
that truly sets me alight…

The clinks of gamblers stacking coins,
the clinks of jailers making noise.
The swish of a final dance's twirling dress,
the swish of a final second's nothing but net.

The gulps of a drowning man fallen into the sea,
the gulps of a girl losing faith in humanity.
The silence that comes when the battle is won,
the silence that comes when the lies have been spun.

Our bodies meet in a passionless display
and I imagine that I am anywhere but here,
in the cold arms of a man who once set me alight.

—in a big empty house

her legs are goalposts, frozen to the ground,
both teams on offense.

please. miss. please. miss. please. miss. please.

the ball sails in a golden arc, seconds away
from bringing life to waiting stadium.

the crowd roars, half in outrage,
the rest with relief.

they carry the players off the field, and soon
the floodlights follow.

she is left in darkness.

—the wrong kind of football

is the descendant of broken beer bottles
that much different from the heir
of cold hard cash?
neither have been truly loved,
but both have solace
to keep them warm for the night.

they meet in a bar.

—trailer avenue

isn't it a pity when
your spotless sheets are washed again
sterile and clean against your will
now a white flag as you set sail

through an ocean of your own making
cross this off as dreams invading
under a sun you wish would set
as your heart melts through the bed

before the rest of your body
could even cross
before you're ready to be lonely
and lost

isn't it a pity when
your speckless cheeks are stained again
and again
and again
and again

—catching seas, sailing the z's

2. forgotten,

DOOR JAM

paradise turns to ash
     and relaxation turns to wrath
     when i spend my life chasing the eternal carat
               even mummified i'd climb that pyramid
                    with the greatest of pharaohs buried beneath it
                                   determined to join them
                                   determined to beat them
                         inching my way to the silver door…
               then the gold…
          then platinum…
diamond...

You can't use sticks and stones
if you intend to hit your mark.
And we can't lose our voices if
we never had one from the start.
How can I be a ghost
when my life was an echo
of something I never saw?

Is life my fatal flaw?

—skin & bone

you were the first to tell me
that i had a way with words.
that i reminded you of the silver screen
and the bars of your favorite song.

but i was the first to tell you
no
because you reminded me
of bars too.

—some bridges were meant to be burned

We Used To Be Best Buddies

to the snowman i built
when i was five
don't worry, you'll never stop
being my friend.
all those years of
shaping and building
had you standing in all your glory,
didn't it?
with snowflake lashes
and eyes made from
the coal santa gave me.
i wonder,
do you ever think of me?
i promise i think of you.

TRICKS

If I were a ghost, I would not find reason to complain.

Passing through random walls, random people, random memories being etched into existence. A witness to life, a spectator to evolution, but never an active participant, unable to suffer at its troughs. I suppose I could never truly experience the peaks of life either, but why would it matter a bit when I can simply float above it all, higher than any cloud nine? Sure, I'd be lonely, but at the end of the day isn't everyone? At least I'm a little more transparent about it.

What do we live for,
If not the promise of more?

A ghost is a wisp of its former self. A ghost does not need more, because they have already lived. They have gained enough, and lost it all. The very nature of human beings, the inescapable law of *more*; I see through it. The real trouble is living with the enlightened lie in an ocean of hollow truth.

So no, if I were a ghost, I'd hardly complain.

there's less to unravel when
simplicity is key.
we weaved a web, then pondered on
our immortality.

—spidermen

Denmark's Tragedy

By the bank, a puppy yips and feasts on flowers,
Unaware of your gemstone irises a few splashes away,
Clear as glass in a winter storm.

Moss starts to adorn your dress made of clouds and fairy wings,
Your nose just above the water, morning dew freckling your cheeks,
Hair blossoming like fireworks.

You sway to the hum of dragonflies, the melancholy sweep of their wings
A funeral march. You glow in the sun, sparkling beneath a pool of tears,
So divine you start to see a god.

Speak, and you shall be heard, allotted flute of the heavens.
Sing, and we shall pay you mind, avenge your every stolen breath.
……why, nary a sigh.

Not the Vampires!

I head to the roof,
All paths led to this view.
The war wages on but my battle is lost,
And oh, what a battle it was.

A step forward. Twenty steps back.
A running start. A bird, plane, Superman!
The jolt is a rush, my bones unlock,
My legs are jello, no other purpose but to fall.

I hit the ground running. I stumble. I crumble.
And yet. I sit up? I stand up? I start to walk?
I search for the joke, strain to hear laughter.
I only hear the angel's choir.

An ache in my spine
And a bruise on my face,
New eyes I've been given,
The world's been replaced.

I'm swirling white in a black ether,
Burning bright in a spangled chasm.
God's gentle tears turned to shipwrecking storms.
Caught in their fears, trapped in their heads,

I'll never be hopeless again.

There's a dream in my bones,
A spirit instilled.
When the masses start crying
I'm barely perturbed.

Very soon, I hear about that morning decree:
Our garlic crops are dead.
The smell will smother,
Then never be smelt again. I laugh.

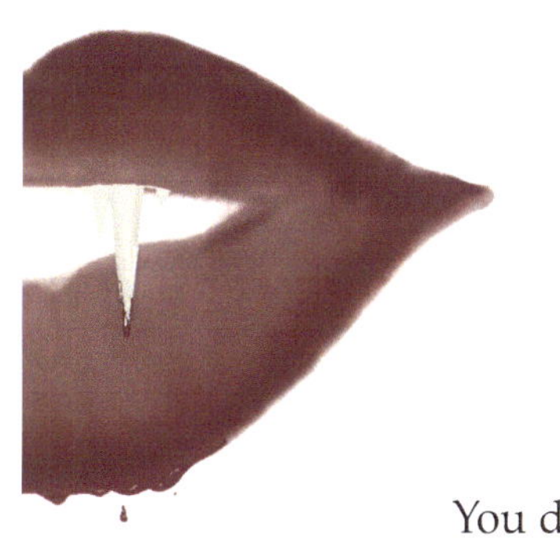

Worry not about the vampires,
I'll stake them through the heart.
My blood courses faster than
Casually flicked darts.

You don't understand, this is serious, they said.
This means there will be no more garlic bread.

I head to the roof again.

the world
kaleidoscopes
before my eyes
and if it's
a hologram
i think
i'd die

it is neither laziness
nor comfy privilege
for one to stop & rest.
you can take a break
while scaling a cliff
and still
be hanging on for dear life.

                    —the key to survival

LILITH

He reminds you of morning breath,
of the birth of mankind.
I'd rather be your dying stars,
the eve to your dawn of time.

They banished me from heaven and earth
yet my garden grows and thrives.
The sun is bound to weep when he sees
your fingers between my thighs.

The angels let their feet touch soil,
they cease their endless flight
just to breathe you in, offer you gifts
in exchange for your delicate light.

An English rose, exquisitely petaled,
the last of your kind.
I burned to ash in the aftermath
of your sapphire mind.

But I'd have more luck turning leaves in the fall
or gazing through blindfolds at a crystal ball
than keeping you by my side, for all of time, crown of fire,
a queen of these desolate pits of desire.

Forever a sin, my seven deadly grins,
the highway was rough, his stairway of bliss
a bone to my ribs, now murder in my heart.
Anything but this, please, anything but this.

You danced with the Devil, but the thrill rots and festers.
Like lovers in history, like the legacy of my ancestors,
you fade before my eyes, the hook has found the fish.
The serpent coils, a mortal with a death wish.

Oh, island of Evangeline, that place I'll never find.
No, I'll never be satisfied.

BOXCUTTER

First position is full of possibilities,
meant to test her paragon abilities.
It's a fine line, to prevent the fatal tilt
on a tightrope of the finest spiders' silk.

The ghost of scissors tracing her spine,
she toes the line, building up her shrine.
And to be quite candid,
the music turned vapid a lifetime ago.

The audience cries, she doesn't mind.
Onstage, the world is black and white.
She leaps, and while arching her back,
she starts to crack.

Failing hard to stay low, staying on her tiptoes,
Bound by a pretty bow, she tightens, then snaps.
The swan becomes a bitter crow, now coal black.

The audience loses their minds.
They scream encore, let roses fly.
The audience might be color-blind.

Arms poised for flight, knees poised to grovel.
Shining all her life, but with shiny pretty baubles
comes a raven's premonition. It's coming, fleeting
feet fleeing. Tragedy chases her ambition.

She gets into fifth position.

PIE HIGH

the truth lies within, like flesh borne from seeds
kept free in the dark, great pomegranate tree

the wines of regret, a craving to swallow
it drips through a cavern, flows true in a hollow

the quill and its patron, one condemns the other
to a life of bare scratches, rare dents and dreams to smother

the silence was silver, turned golden with time
replacing our teeth, leaving cuts in our spines

ah, pizza's arrived.

the cheap fluorescents
have turned your skin
a tinted rose,
and the dandelions
have formed
a galaxy
of their own

   —moondance

do you miss it?
when you were young enough to bet against a god
and win? do you miss the stretch of your self-righteous grin?

when, as you drew near, people scattered like ashes,
with every hurricane flutter of your lashes
a felled tree, could you hide your glee?

when you could beam at the heavens
with a mouthful of pins hidden in your purse,
and not be struck dead like the countless before you,

that was the prime of your youth. do you miss it?
as you begin to draw that heart-stopping breath,
will you reminisce?

—demigods

RUMPELSTILTSKIN

is there much in a name
that cannot be changed
should the rose start to sour and wilt?

is there much to be sold
with a gift of fool's gold
should it glitter despite all the guilt?

is there much to adore
if the promise of more
should be hubris that rusts in the light?

is there much to be said
when the oath's good and dead
will you tell me that you're in the right?

i thought you might.

TEMPLES

there was always a rule at every temple:
step over the threshold, never directly on.
we soon made a game of it, practicing all year
fancy cartwheels, backflips, leaps and twirls,
just to earn bragging rights on sacred soil.

tock, tock, tock, tock goes the ritual drums,
my heart forced to follow its rhythm.
i try to take a breath, but muster a wheeze,
the incense slithering like snakes up my nose,
dripping their poison into my eyes.

my parents on either side, squint and glare
at every shuffle, every sigh. that was another rule:
no boredom allowed. and that monk may be a bitch,
but she deserves your utmost respect.

my grandmother's devoted, and to her i'm devout,
so i kneel like she does, hands clasped in prayer,
eyes peeking at the candy bowl that sits on the table.
she beams when she sees me wearing the beads
that she loved me enough to carefully bless.

we arrive at my favorite, lady of compassion,
goddess of mercy, the mother who could've been.
we bow before her, the scent of lotus in the air.
and in my head, unbidden, unasked for,
comes a soundless remark that
her boobs are smaller than i remember.

3. lost.

MARIPOSA

Opening eyes, and a cry, for you know that the
woman's throne is a stool, and the fools get the gold.
It glitters while we dance to their melody, wax figures
marching to a candle that has burned for centuries.

Your voice reduced to scraps of cloth, to shoulder blades,
your wishes held in place by a man's wandering hands.
Your iridescence is attracting the moths, beware
of the gentleman's stare, of the nobleman's gaze.

We hate the taste, our gums still used to our mother's bosom.
What a shame, to look between two innocents
and pick the one without the heart, without the hurt,
without the skirt, without the consequence.

Hate the stinging gravel, hate the pardon gavel.
Wings unfurled, then clamped in the jaws of a cat.
They don't look back, drawn to the curls of a child,
they call her delinquent juvenile, rather than

a butterfly
pinned on its back.

why do i keep
squeezing this tube
of toothpaste
when i know
there's nothing left
and for what?
it's a toothache
nothing short of a
visit to the dentist
can help
but it's fine
i have my toothpaste here
if i could just
get
some
out of this tube
i'll be fine

Life Support

i may have gone
and confused myself again—
when did i become
a sob story, condensed to four lines:

"her unhinged, and yet,
expected behavior
leaves their heads hanging,
they pray for a savior."

i mean, i have *friends*.
i have food, and a bed.
i guess above all,
i have awareness, i have dread.

now, won't i lose it all
if i choose pity instead?

I chased freedom while
everything else fell behind.
So erratic, so faithfully nomadic,
That even life itself failed to catch up.

But as I ran in a race I thought I was winning,
My dreams turned to dust underfoot.
I tripped over roots of my own design.

And now,
I am groot.

I set my brushes on the barren ground.
Don't worry, I'll paint over the cracks
as soon as *it* comes. Of course,
that's easel for me to say.

In the meantime,
I cavort with my enemies, and the panthers,
and the mice. After all, we wait in line
for the very same thing:

Something to justify the blood in our noses,
something to fuel our need for purpose.
Above all, it gives us rose-colored sunglasses,
rose-scented perfumes, rose-flavored ices…

And when it comes,
I'll embrace it like Mrs. Death
did her husband, like stars with arms
far more open than any father's.

And it will come, at the moment we least expect it.
In the blink of an eye we'll be encased in molds
of silver and gold, no longer scum of the earth.
Yes, it will come,
it will come like water that is damned;

that is to say, not at all.

—Cracks of my own making

i'm the trustworthy type,
the kind who sits and listens
to all your problems.
you can trust me with your life
and you'll never ever find
a knife in your back.
....you're not an owl, are you?

—whooo me?

you shouldn't fear.
your sparkle won't disappear
off the edge of that
endless waterfall.
the wetness of your tears
are sea salt chandeliers;
they make the light in your eyes
that much more
worthy
of attention.

—crybaby

Can someone else take the wheel for a while?
I fear I've dragged myself into an abyss.
My drive has done nothing
but drive me to madness.
Other's successes
are either my regret
or a new goal to twist
into the disapproving curve
of my mother's lips. Oh,
my successes?
Don't make me laugh.

                    —a parasite's tale

CHANGE

i would never change myself for anyone
edit my persona to fit your tastes
this peer pressure haze is no more than a phase
i will not change

nothing but a tweak to my hairstyle
nothing but a little glitter in my smile
photoshop the fashion
autotune the accent

now i have potential to be loved
the mask, it fits like a glove

SARAH,
no one likes a snitch.
The rat that skitters through the gutters
while the falcons soar and the bears snarl
with sharpened teeth. Your words aren't as sharp
as you'd like to think. They're blunt like your head,
heavy with consequences and the jealousy
that burns your heart out. Desperate for
the eye of the Devil, you've doomed yourself.
You've threaded the needle.
One pull and your life is unraveled.
No one likes a snitch, but no one hates them either,
because one way or another, they all take the wrong step
and are never heard from again.

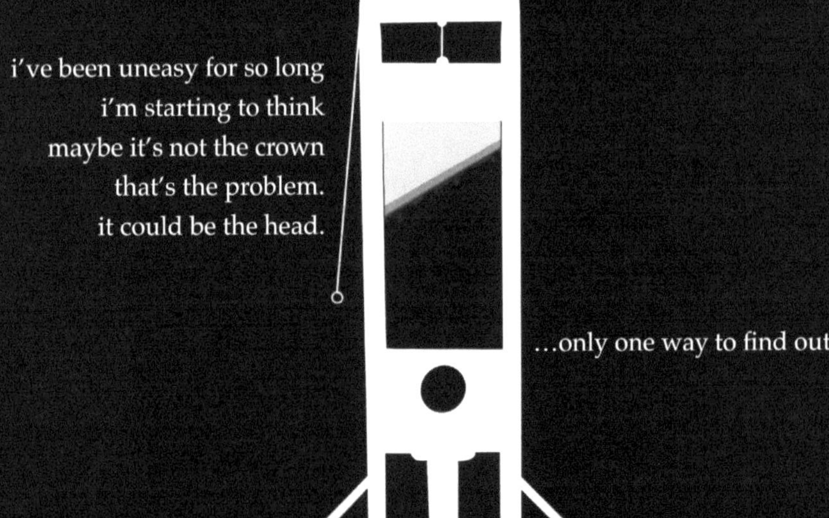

i've been uneasy for so long
i'm starting to think
maybe it's not the crown
that's the problem.
it could be the head.
...only one way to find out.
—off with it

VELVET

you're not who you seem, are you?
what big shoes you must think you have
to stand in my path,
all while crushing the violets underfoot.
even worse,
your fate is wrapped around my wrist
like the scratchiest twine,
as tempting to cut as the skin that lays beneath.
i know the secret you've been fighting to keep,
and isn't it ironic
that it's all about me?
my little red headband…
hoodie…
hat…
my grandmother died
with no one to hold her hand.
and what paleness, snow white
that the blood might flow darker.
you insult her,
a child's name on your tongue,
bile on mine,
enough that i forget to breathe.
yet you continue to say it
again and again and again and again
and i can't stop you, can i?
for i am exactly as i seem:
a child.

i've never heard true silence
but i've yearned it all my life
and i'm not the only one
i just know it
why else do people kill themselves
if not to get
that little slice of quiet
no sugar, no butter
no strings attached
and what about the ones who live?
well
they're just here
hoping to get a taste of
that cake they were promised

—just desserts

We Used To Be Best Buddies (Edited)

to the snowman i built
when i was five,
i wish you never stopped
being my friend.
but i can't go back in time
to the snowflake lashes
and eyes made of
the buttons from my coat.
i chose the hourglass sand
and its warmth between my toes.
so, i can't go back in time
but i wonder,
do you ever think of me?
i promise i think of you.

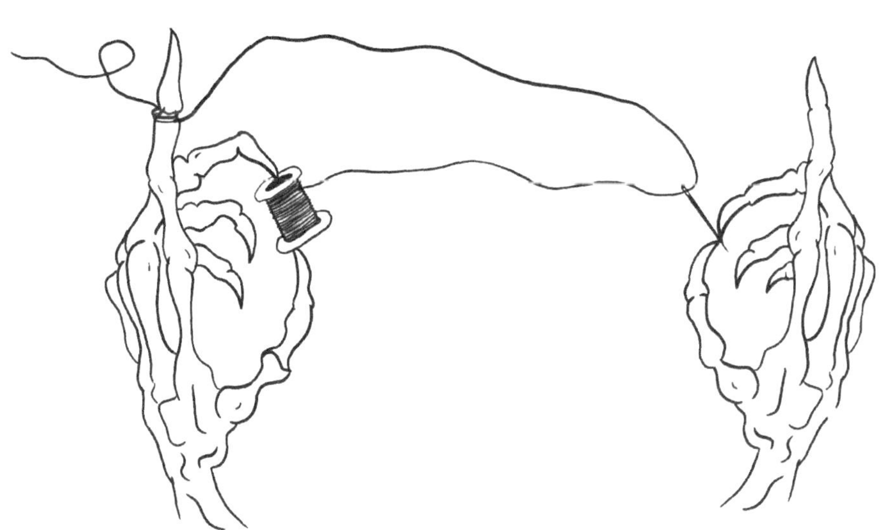

HIRAETH

one summer night, i was born tone deaf
but with ghostly lyrics in my head.
haunting me, a creature of rhythm, loyal to man,
taunting the heart that beats in my hands.

i remember that summer, and every summer after that.
the cold of my fingers, and the ice in my lap
as i sculpted story after story, family after family,
vision lost, voice unlocked, venom spat rather cannily.

how could i not embrace the noose, that old medieval tie,
when i spent all my sunlit life fleeing from the dark of night?
it was always sharp, pressed against my skin,
nails scratching, tapping against walls closing in.

the sticky sweet summer rain, the curtain capes,
pink lemonade, turned sour with shadows
dropping like bodies, punching like hail,
childhood gone sallow, memories turned pale.

the nostalgia was fake, it was often replaced
by pictures printed off the internet.
i remember swimming pools at 3am
and the teeth of sharks come to try again.

one summer night, i was borne to Death
with the angel chorus in my head.
i was not free, i remember no glee, but recall the trust
as the silence of light was finally afforded to us.

Do you remember when you were young, and followed your mom into a store? She tells you not to touch anything. You pretend to listen until the second she turns her head.

Your fingers running down the sides of every little trinket you can get your hands on. Fluttering, ghosting, trailing. Searching for the sign, the lightning strike. Waiting for the dent, the groove, the telltale click. The moment your nails graze just the right spot, and your mind is unlocked, your soul set free.

Sometimes, it slips. Butter fingers, sticky fingers.

You try to move on, tapping a staccato beat against your knee, drumming at an empty page, hovering, poised, over brand-new keys. Waiting patiently for that perfect pull of the bow, drawing that velvet sound, sweet and low, drawing from a chunk of wood a perfect melody.

And then it retreats, ready to be found once again.

4.

...found.